Take Me to Buc-ee's Please!

By

Alexia Tennent

Copyright © 2019 Alexia Tennent

All rights reserved

No part of this publication may be reproduced, stored or transmitted in any form or by any means, electronic, mechanical, photocopying, recording, scanning, or otherwise without written permission from the publisher. It is illegal to copy this book, post it to a website, or distribute it by any other means without permission

ISBN: 978-1-951844-02-8

This book is dedicated to Nathan and Natalie

Whoever said everything is bigger in Texas was standing right outside Buc-ee's when they thought of it.

As far as the eyes can see to the left or right, there are gas pumps and cars sitting at the pumps. Once in a while, we have to drive around to find an available pump. I don't mind. I am always happy to go to Buc-ee's.

Where else can you find over 100 pumps at one gas station?

When we go to the pump on the right end, it means we are going to the car wash. Oh yeah! I love the car wash. If you buy the car wash at the same time that you fill up, there is a discount per gallon. Gas is already cheaper at Buc-ee's. It is a win-win situation.

I could see the car wash in the distance from the back seat of the car. I couldn't wait to get in there. It reminds me of pulling into Penn Station in New York City. This is the longest car wash in the world at 255 ft.

Oh, the simple pleasures of life!

We get "the works." We enter the code we purchased at the gas pump and select free vacuum. Then we wait.

When it is our turn, the gate opens to let us through. I get more excited the closer we get to the car wash.

The attendant signals for us to approach. Mom puts the car in neutral and reclines her seat so she can enjoy the view too. She says it is relaxing.

Finally, we are inside! Mom retracts the cover to the panoramic moon roof so I can see everything from the back seat. It is marvelous!

The Buc-ee's logo beaming through never gets old.

Neither does the colorful foam covering the car. The view from inside the car is amazing!

Next, it is time to dry and shine. The blow dryers are so powerful, it seems they were intended to blow the car away. I love it!

Ahhh! All good things must come to an end... until next week!

If you think the outside is impressive, check out the inside! A trip to Buc-ee's is priceless. It is worth more than a hundred trips to McDonald's. Here, all the meals are happy. Where do I begin?

We live 8 minutes west of one Buc-ee's and 10 minutes east of another. There is another Buc-ee's 23 minutes south of us and only 5 minutes from my piano class. I am one lucky girl. When my friends come over for play dates, we go to the park and we go to Buc-ee's.

Once we get inside, we go nuts!

First, we must wash our hands. The restrooms here are awesome. They are the cleanest and nicest restrooms I have ever seen in a public place.

The entrance to the restroom looks more like home than a gas station.

There are dozens of stalls going all the way around. Great place for hide and seek if it is not busy. Each stall has hand sanitizer on the wall. There is also another sanitizer for wiping the toilet seat just in case you make a mess. The cleaning lady here must be really good at her job. If I didn't know better I would think it was my mom.

I get the x-large cup of ice for my bottled water. It's only 53 cents.

Then I ask mom if I can get a fruit cup. It is one of my favorites.

I usually get a kolache too. There are several to choose from.

Mom prefers a brisket sandwich

We both love the world famous jerky.

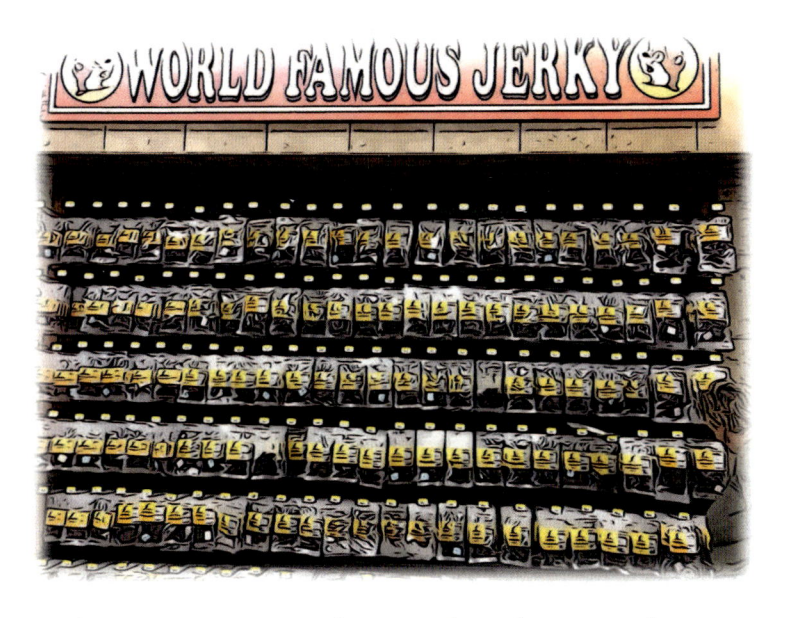

So does everyone else. Jerky this good deserves a wall to itself. There are so many to choose from.

I have not tried the beaver nuggets yet. But I heard they are good. I am not a big fan of caramel. There is something for everyone at Buc-ee's.

Chocolate and caramel

Powder candy

Meat and cheese trays

Sandwiches

Salads

Jellies and preserves

Wines

Coffee and hot chocolate

Pretzels

Candles, bath and body products

Purses

Plush toys

Children's books

Souvenirs

Clothes

Grills

Backyard and tailgating stuff

Household

Automotive

Jewelry

Seasonal items

27

Buc-ee's is one of my favorite places to go. They have some of the most unusual things I have ever seen, such as candied jalapeño, pickled quail eggs, taffy, gummies and fudges with flavors I have never seen anywhere else. If you can think of it, they probably sell it. If you never thought of it, they probably have it. There is so much to do and see at Buc-ee's. I always want to go there. It never gets old. Buc-ee's is my happy place! I have visited many of the Buc-ee's locations while on road trips with my mom. I can't wait until Buc-ee's is everywhere across the country. Everyone deserves the Buc-ee's experience. Did I mention they have clean restrooms?

Made in the USA
Las Vegas, NV
17 June 2025